RED STEAGALL
NEW AND SELECTED POEMS

Red Steagall
New and Selected Poems

TCU Press
Fort Worth, Texas

TCU Texas Poets Laureate Series

Library of Congress Cataloging-in-Publication Data

Steagall, Red.
  Red Steagall : new and selected poems/edited by Billy Bob Hill
    p. cm. -- (TCU Texas poets laureate series ; 2)
  ISBN-13: 978-0-87565-341-9 (alk. paper)
  ISBN-10: 0-87565-341-3 (alk. paper)
  I. Hill, Billy Bob. II. Title.

PS3569.T33735R43 2007
811'.6--dc22
                              2006039070

DEDICATION

I DEDICATE THIS BOOK

TO MY SOUL-MATE

AND BEST FRIEND,

MY WIFE,

GAIL

TABLE OF CONTENTS

Introduction

The abilities of Red Steagall the musician, both in performance and songwriting, are generally known. His poetry is not as well known because poetry is, in our age, not as popular as song.

That is not to say that he does not have a readership; he has a number of poetry books and is the current Texas Poet Laureate. Readers have noticed his gift for storytelling and his first-hand knowledge of the American West. Perhaps, *Red Steagall: New and Selected Poems* will help a larger readership understand the other good qualities of his writings.

His poems have their roots in a number of traditions. For one, he crafts verse in the tradition of cowboy songs, not a surprising fact when one considers that he is a musician and a cowboy, if a cowboy with a college degree. But in "The Memories in Grandmother's Trunk," Steagall goes beyond his ranching days and backward in time into ancestral memory.

They came in a wagon from St. Jo, Missouri.
Grandmother was seven years old.
I remember she said she walked most of the way
Through the rain, and the mud, and the cold.

She saw the Comanche. They came into camp—
Not the savage she'd seen in her dreams.
They were ragged and pitiful, hungry, and cold
Begging for salt pork and beans.

He is hardly the first Texan to blend regional folk art with artistic poetry. Although some meaningful differences exist between Red Steagall's body of work and that of Laurence Chittenden, one reminds me of the other.

I would guess that Grace Noll Crowell, who served as the Texas Poet Laureate in our Centennial year, sold more poetry books than any other Texan in history. I would then guess that Laurence Chittenden would place second with *Ranch Verses*.

After moving from his native New Jersey, Larry Chittenden (1862-1934) wrote poems while riding herd on his uncle's ranch along the Old McKenzie Trail. Chittenden became nationally known as "The Poet Ranchman," and Putnam and Sons reprinted *Ranch Verses* fifteen times.

Steagall's poetry collections also remind me of other Southwestern books. Chittenden's *Ranch Verses* was first published in 1893. Editor and folksong-catcher, John A. Lomax first published his anthology, *Cowboy Songs and Other Frontier Ballads* in 1910. It was through this scholarly songbook that many Americans became aware of "Git Along, Little Dogies" and "Home on the Range." I see a similar authenticity in Red Steagall's poetry, playing off of oral tradition.

In 1950, folklorist and novelist William A. Owens published *Texas Folk Songs*. This compilation included old ballads, some of which had traveled across the American Plains and some across the Atlantic West. Along with "Come, All Young Cowboys," one finds "The Oxford Girl," whose melody and lyrics predate the Mayflower. In the introduction to *Texas Folk Songs*, William Owens explains: "Anglo-Saxon, Anglo-American, Anglo-Texan; each of these terms is an extension of the preceding—one parent to another, just as European is parent to all three..."

People of Celtic heritage are not often thrilled with being classified as Anglo. Fort Worth writer, Joyce Gibson Roach, who knows Red Steagall better than I do, more clearly defines this lineage:

> Celtic stock—the Irish and the Scots—all but raced for the wilds of the frontier. In no group was the folk singing, poetry reciting, and tale telling penchant stronger than in descendants of the ancient Celts who moved into the South and then by wagon, horseback, and afoot to Texas and beyond. Red Steagall (Steagall is an Irish name, although it isn't fair, perhaps, to make too much of it) by genetics, interest, and disposition, recites and sings a modern version of an ancient form. The singers and poets before Red did the same.

To me, given this literary line, Steagall's work is reminiscent of that of Robert Burns. In the poems of the beloved Scot, one finds use of dialect, a fluctuation between poetry and song, a flowing conversational charm, a sense of whimsy, and a sense of place. There is something in "McCorkle and the Wire" that calls up "Tam O'Shanter." As with Robert Burns, the Texas Poet Laureate echoes oral tradition within his personal art.

The other evening, I watched a PBS documentary about ranch life in Texas, and Red Steagall served as the show's narrator. Clearly, he is associated with the cattle culture and has a readership that follows publications on that topic. However, one need not know a John Blocker Loop from a Barlow knife to enjoy this collection. The winning elements in *Red Steagall: New and Selected Poems* can speak to many.

The Memories in Grandmother's Trunk

They came in a wagon from St. Jo, Missouri.
Grandmother was seven years old.
I remember she said she walked most of the way
Through the rain, and the mud and the cold.

She saw the Comanche, they came into camp—
Not the savage she'd seen in her dreams.
They were ragged and pitiful, hungry, and cold
Begging for salt pork and beans.

They staked out a claim at the cross timbers breaks
Where the big herds went north to the rail.
One day a cowpuncher gave her a calf
Too young to survive on the trail.

Their Jersey cow gave more milk than they needed
The calf grew up healthy and strong.
She staked him that fall in the grass by the creek
And pampered him all winter long.

In April her daddy rode into Fort Worth
With her calf on the end of his rope.
He traded her prize for a red cedar trunk
That she filled full of memories and hope.

I found grandmother's trunk hidden under a bed
In a back room where she used to sleep.
I've spent the whole morning reliving her youth
Through the trinkets that she fought to keep.

There's the old family Bible, yellowed and worn
On the first page was her family tree.
She'd traced it clear back to the New England coast
And the last entry she made was me.

I unfolded a beautiful star pattern quilt
In the corner she cross-stitched her name.
I wonder how many children it kept safe and warm
From the cold of the West Texas plain.

There's a tattered old picture that says "Mom, I Love You"
Tho' faded, there's a young soldier's face.
And a medal of honor the government sent
When he died in a faraway place.

A cradleboard covered with porcupine quills
Traded for salt pork and beans,
Was laying on top of a ribbon that read
Foard County Rodeo Queen.

Dried flowers pressed in a book full of poems
A card with this message engraved,
To my darlin' wife on our 25th year
And some old stamps my grandfather saved.

Of course there are pictures of her daddy's folks
They sure did look proper and prim.
I reckon if they were to come back to life
We'd look just as funny to them.

Grandmother's life seemed so simple and slow
But the world started changin' too soon.
She heard the first radio, saw the first car,
And lived to see men on the moon.

Life on this planet is still marching on
And I hope that my grandchildren see,
My side of life through the trinkets I've saved
The way grandmother's trunk does for me.

1988

THE CODE OF THE WEST HASN'T CHANGED

The horsetrap is empty, the saddle shed's gone,
The gate barely hangs on the post.
The road to the big house is covered with weeds
A dead cottonwood moans like a ghost.

The people who ranched here and called this place home
Are pasturing on some other ground.
Maybe they've gone on to greater rewards
Or drouthed out and moved into town.

Whatever the reason, there's nobody here
And it looks like it's been a long while
Since anyone cared if this place was alive
But I can look back with a smile.

'Cause I can remember the twenty-odd years
That I rode for this outfit with pride.
Shore 'nuff good people, they treated us fair
And gave us good horses to ride.

And there was young Rusty, we called him the kid
Tho' he wasn't much younger than me.
He was killed in the cow work at Willow Springs Camp
When a bronc run him under a tree.

And the Triangle roan, when he was a colt
He would try ya each time you got on.
But once he quit buckin' and I got him lined out
Was the best friend that I've ever known.

There's the bed of the wagon we took into town
When they throwed the big dance in the fall.
One time I rode horseback and drank too much hootch
Like to never got back home at all.

We'd tie up the reins, let the team have its head
And while Murdock would spin us a yarn,
We'd sit in the wagon and have a good time
While the team took us back to the barn.

They've fenced the big pasture and divvied it up
Into places that won't run a cow.
It shore breaks my heart to remember it then
And see what they've done to it now.

The big thicket's gone off the cedar top flat
Where the wagon would stay for a week.
I shore miss old camp cookie's sourdough bread
At the roundup on Cottonwood Creek.

I wonder what happened to Curley and Bill
Cotton and Cody and Slim.
And Murdock, the wagon boss, where has he gone?
I shore took a likin' to him.

I reckon they're workin' on some other range
And their horses may not buck as bad.
I bet they're still cowboy'n, at least in their minds,
And relivin' the fun that we had.

I'm sure that the years have reshuffled my cards,
And the hand that I play's rearranged.
but I'll die believin' we had a good time
And that the code of the west hasn't changed.

1989

A DUSTY COTTON FIELD

I often thought of leaving home
When I was 'bout half grown.
Saddle up my trusty steed;
Head out for parts unknown.

An eighty-acre cotton farm
Was not my cup of tea.
I dreamed of working cattle
On the open grassy sea.

But something always held me there.
I think I understood
That it would break my mama's heart
If I took off for good.

And tho' I hated cotton fields
And dust and balky mules,
I also knew my daddy had
An ironclad set of rules.

"If you don't work then you don't eat,"
Was what my daddy said.
I often thought he's kiddin',
But I'se craving beans and bread.

I didn't buck the badger
On a gamble he was right.
I figured I would starve to death
In case I lost the fight.

And now that I am older
I look back on all those years.
I realize that it was more than
Just my mama's tears

That took away my wanderlust
And made me stay at home.
It wasn't daddy's ironclad rules
That killed my urge to roam.

Was all that love they gave me.
It was all that time they spent
To make sure I had all the tools
So I could make a dent

In a world that I would call my own
When they won't be around.
That's why I'm able now to plant
And plow unbroken ground.

Tho' I've become a cowboy
And my dreams are truly real,
I know I learned to hold my own
In dusty cotton fields.

I know that mama's tender love
And daddy's firm, strong hand
Have molded me and made me
Be a better, stronger man.

I wouldn't trade that cotton field
For satchels full of gold.
I wouldn't trade a balky mule
For jewels and wealth untold.

'Cause all the things I learned from them
Are keeping me on track;
But I don't miss the heat and dust
And I ain't goin' back.

1999

Bedroll

There's a hole in the wagonsheet big as my head
Where coosie run under a tree.
Last week it rained and poured right in that hole
Probably nobody noticed but me.

'Cause that was the mornin' I jingled the horses
It rained and my bed was just fine.
But it was the first one to go in the wagon
And the rest of 'em stacked up on mine.

Last winter we put a new floor in that wagon
We planked it with tongue and groove oak.
She's tight as a drum and won't leak a drop
So the bed on the bottom got soaked.

Now canvas is good about turnin' the dew
As long as it's stretched the right way.
But I guess something happens, it sorta breaks down
Sittin' in water all day.

Your bed's usually warm and a nice place to be
A cowpuncher's private domain.
But it's colder 'n hell in a bedroll that's wet
You're better off out in the rain.

So I put on my slicker and sat by the fire
Burned all the dry wood in the stack.
The fire made me drowsy—once I dozed off
And woke up in the mud, on my back.

Just before sunup I crawled in that bed
Couldn't sleep 'cause my feet were so numb.
Then coosie was cussin' I burned all his wood
So I got up and gathered him some.

Now I ain't one to argue and create a fuss
And I don't get my head in a fog.
But it's taken a week for me to get her dried out
And last night I slept like a log.

This mornin' it's thunderin' and carryin' on
It's already startin' to rain.
And I know for a fact coosie ain't fixed that hole
And I ain't goin' through that again.

Everyone's saddled and ready to ride
Except me and I'll be here a while.
I want to make sure when they load up the wagon
My bed's on the top of the pile.

1989

mccorkle anD THe wire

McCorkle rode into the Whiskey Flat Camp
On a lathered-up walleyed blue roan.
He was talkin' in circles, clean out of his head,
And shakin' right down to the bone.

We made him get down—Billy Joe took his reins,
Tom offered a nip o' the jug.
He sat on my bedroll and asked for a chew—
I give him a cut of my plug.

He said, "Early this mornin' I was out ridin' fence,
About six—it was just gettin' light.
I was checkin' for breaks from the rim of Bates Draw,
When I seen a blood curdlin' sight.

"This feller was laying up under his horse.
They both was tied up in the wires.
Neither was movin'—I thought they was dead.
I reached in my bag for the pliers.

"The cowboy looked up and said, 'Give me a hand.
I think I'm all broken inside.'
I took out my cutter and worked on the wire.
'Fore I finished, the cowpuncher died.

"I got on my horse and rode straight into camp.
His dyin' shore gave me a scare.
Could I get you podnahs to give me some help,
And bury that feller out there?"

I asked if his clothes were those out of the past,
If his kack was a Visalia tree,
If the shank of his bit had a US Rosette,
And the brand on his horse was a three.

McCorkle looked like he had swallered his tongue.
He stood up and reached for his gun.
"How did you know? Did he ride by the camp?
This ain't no time to be pokin' fun."

I looked at McAlister. He turned away.
We'd both heard this story before.
"It seems that some puncher a long time ago
Is still tryin' to settle a score.

"Late in the '90s they fenced off the grass.
Most people thought it was wrong.
Some carried fence pliers, made their own laws,
But the open range era was gone.

"This feller was bad about cutting a fence,
Paid no mind at all to the law.
The ranchers had taken about all they could take.
They set up a trap in the draw.

"A group of their punchers hid out in the brush.
The fence was stretched ready to break.
They had purposely not tied the wire to the posts.
When they cut it, it coiled like a snake.

"Four strands of bobwire a hundred foot long,
Like a thousand knives flashed through the air.
This feller had just gotten down from his horse
When the wire hit and parted his hair.

"The night air was filled with the sound of his screams.
The coyote was captured, and then
They rode off and left him to die on his own,
Laughin', 'He won't cut fences again.'

"For ninety-odd years now he keeps coming back,
And ropes in some feller like you.
He knows you can't cut him free all by yourself,
And you'll go for some help—ain't that true?"

McCorkle don't buy it. He gets on his horse.
We wait till he rides out of sight.
We follered him out but we gave him some room,
'Cause McCorkle is ready to fight.

When we got to the rim he was white as a ghost
Said, "I'm sorry I called you a liar."
From the top of Bates Draw, we could see every strand
And not one single break in the wire.

McCorkle pulled out, and we ain't seen him since.
We hired a new man in the fall.
We're still out workin' the Whiskey Flat range,
Just as tho' nothin' happened at all.

Pete says, "McCorkle's run off the deep end.
He's crazy and moves around slow.
He drinks lots of whiskey and keeps to himself,
And his hair's turned as white as the snow."

1990

Born TO THIS Land

I've kicked up the hidden mesquite roots and rocks
From the place where I spread out my bed.
I'm layin' here lookin' at a sky full of stars
With my hands folded up 'neath my head.

Tonight there's a terrible pain in my heart
Like a knife, it cuts jagged and deep.
This evening the windmiller brought me the word
That my granddaddy died in his sleep.

I saddled my gray horse and rode out to a hill
Where when I was a youngster of nine,
My granddaddy said to me, "Son, this is ours,
All of it, yours, your daddy's, and mine.

"Son, my daddy settled here after the war
That new tank's where his house used to be.
He wanted to cowboy and live in the West
Came to Texas from east Tennessee.

"The longhorns were wild as the deer in them breaks.
With a long rope he caught him a few.
With the money he made from trailin' 'em north,
Son, he proved up this homestead for you.

"The railroad got closer, they built the first fence
Where the river runs through the east side.
When I was a button we built these corrals
Then that winter my granddaddy died.

"My father took over and bought up more range
With good purebreds he improved our stock.
It seems that the windmills grew out of the ground
Then the land got as hard as a rock.

"Then during the dust bowl we barely hung on,
The north wind tried to blow us away.
It seemed that the Lord took a likin' to us
He kept turnin' up ways we could stay.

"My daddy grew older and gave me more rein,
We'd paid for most all of the land.
By the time he went on I was running more cows
And your daddy was my right hand man."

His eyes got real cloudy, took off in a trot,
And I watched as he rode out of sight.
'Tho I was a child, I knew I was special
And I'm feelin' that same way tonight.

Not many years later my daddy was killed
On a ship in the South China Sea.
For twenty-odd years now we've made this ranch work
Just two cowboys, my granddad and me.

And now that he's gone, things are certain to change
And I reckon that's how it should be.
But five generations have called this ranch home
And I promise it won't end with me.

'Cause I've got a little one home in a crib
When he's old enough he'll understand,
From the top of that hill I'll show him his ranch
'Cause like me, he was Born to This Land.

1989

THE REAL AMERICA

I've traveled 'cross this country, been in towns from coast
to coast,
Played rodeos and clubs and county fairs.
I look for my America in every place I go.
I find her where her people truly care.

I found her in San Angelo at old Ft. Concho Days,
At Copper Mountain Westfest in the fall,
In Winchester, Virginia, during apple blossom time,
In Cheyenne at the granddad of them all.

It's not impressive buildings or the car the mayor drives.
It's people in her towns that make her tall.
It's caring for each other, being quick to lend a hand,
The pride in people down at city hall.

The Western Heritage Classic in the town of Abilene
Is one that stole my cowboy heart away.
The spirit and the values upon which this country stands
Are things I saw in Abilene today.

While waking down the thoroughfare amongst the milling
throng,
Where western wear is more than just a fad,
I saw the little fellers in their cowboy hats and boots
Tryin' hard to walk and talk just like their dads.

Then down in the arena, all the teams were recognized,
Each cowboy's proud, he's riding for the brand.
He's keen to competition and is loyal to the core,
But always first to lend a helping hand.

When they played the national anthem, every person faced
    the flag,
With hats in hand they sang their souls away.
My heart welled up inside me as I listened to them sing,
I heard the real America today.

The ones who built this country must have been this kind
of folks
No envy, spite, or pride get in the way.
Respect for other people, bein' proud of who you are
Perhaps the world will understand someday.

The backbone of this country is the folks who work the
land
Like raisin' stock or growin' wheat and corn.
They learn responsibility before they learn to walk,
Friends, this is where America was born.

Integrity and honesty are what they teach their young.
You have a chance, be all you dare to be.
I saw no guns or violence, heard no insults, threats, or lies
Just people bein' happy, livin' free.

They have their share of problems, but they face them
    with a smile,
They live life in a simple kind of way.
They dream of a tomorrow, with respect for yesteryear
I saw the real America today.

1994

Deacon and the Dun

Ol' Deacon was a puncher, born a hundred years too late.
A top hand and he sure as hell was tough.
His bed was in a corner, it had been there thirty years.
God help the man who riffled through his stuff.

I'd ridden lots of roundups when he didn't say a thing.
As tho' the words were stickin' in his craw.
Don't know if he was crazy or a woman done him wrong.
I always thot he's hidin' from the law.

Now Deacon cared for horses like no man I've ever known.
He lived to see the babies in the spring.
His favorite was a zebra dun, he raised him from a colt.
The old man pampered Dunny like a king.

Four of us was in the south camp through the winter months,
Me and him and Buck and Billy Joe.
The only thing he ever said to any one of us,
Was who would ride with who and where to go.

We were calvin' heifers in the Palo Duro Breaks.
A norther hit and started spittin' snow.
Was stickin' to the cedar where we rode along the rim,
The valley lay three hundred feet below.

Then Deacon saw a baldy heifer standing on a ledge.
She looked to be about a two-year-old.
Don't know if she was stuck there or she maybe lost her calf.
Was bawling like a banshee in the cold.

So Deacon took old Dunny down a little rocky trail,
I watched the horse and rider disappear.
Then just as I approached the rim, the heifer ducked her head,
And bounded up that trail just like a deer.

Old Dunny tried to step aside and let the heifer pass.
The trail was narrow where they chose to meet.
Now Deacon knew they both would fall if he stayed in his kack,
Without him, Dunny might regain his feet.

Was at that very moment that she saw a little light
Between old Dunny and the canyon wall.
The old man left the saddle like an eagle takes to wing.
I stared in disbelief and watched him fall.

I had to ride the canyon rim until I found a trail.
It took forever pickin' my way down.
I found him by a cottonwood all rolled up in a wad.
Was breathin' but he barely made a sound.

Every single bone was broken, his eyes were all that moved.
He couldn't lift his head up but he tried.
Through splintered teeth he asked me, "Son, did Dunny make
it out?"
I nodded, he just smiled, and then he died.

Now in his stuff we found a dozen stories he had wrote,
'Bout horses he had ridden in his life.
But there was not a mention of his family or his friends.
No indication of a child or wife.

So what we know about him we can still put in my hat.
And tho' his story has a better end,
He could have jumped the other way, let Dunny take the fall,
But Deacon gave his life to save a friend.

1990

THE LAST BUFFALO

I sit at my desk and occasionally glance
At a buffalo skull on the wall—
Was painted by a Hidatsa medicine man.
If the ancient skull could talk at all

He might tell me tales of the great grassy sea
On the bountiful Panhandle Plains,
Or remember the nights 'neath a Montana sky,
Or the cold of the Wind River rains.

He might remember a young Cheyenne warrior
On a spotted horse, how he could ride
Staying abreast of a running fat cow,
With a lance that left death in its stride.

He might remember the hide-huntin' men
And the sound of a buffalo gun,
Or the smell of fresh blood as they died one by one
Until there was no place to run.

The yearly migration of millions of beasts
Made it look like the land was alive.
The wolves took the weak ones, the winter took some,
And the Indian took enough to survive.

The Indian believed the buffalo was his brother,
Like the coyote, the eagle, the wind.
He revered him in story, in song, and in dance,
Was his larder, his shelter, his friend.

His brown hide was used for the teepee and robes.
A shoulder blade made a good hoe.
A paunch held the food for the winter supply,
And a sinew a string for a bow.

Then the Sharp's Big 50 roared over the land,
Till only a few head remained.
The ones that were left either died of old age
Or were captured when they fenced off the plain.

On the railhead at Dodge the great stacks of hides
Were loaded on railcars and then,
While the carcasses rotted and wolves picked the bones,
Cobblers made boots from the skin.

The Comanche went out from the Fort Sill stockade—
For one final hunt on the plain.
They returned to the fort, their destruction
    complete.
They would never hunt buffalo again.

The Sioux and the Cheyenne came into the forts.
They died from disease by the score.
But they still believed that the great massive herds
Would return to the plains as before.

The dream still survives, and in my mind I see
The Comanche still lord of the plain.
But this ancient old skull with its dark, empty eyes
Is the prairie song's saddest refrain.

1988

CLIMBIN' OUT THE OTHER SIDE

I hired on at the wagon, green and wet behind the ears
My job was wranglin' wood for coosie's fire.
Tho' I was short on talent, I was long on grit and guts,
And stuffed plumb full of willin' and desire.

Now the more I'se 'round the cowboys, the more I realized
This is where I really want to be.
I worked as hard as I could work to make the boss a hand,
So when he'd need a cowboy he'd pick me.

Was at the next spring branding when I finally got
    my chance.
The older cowboys helped me pick my string.
They roped a deep red sorrel with the devil in his eyes.
He musta throwed me twenty times that spring.

He taught me how to cowboy, and like J.J. Gibson said,
"You got the makin's; learn to roll your own.
If someone rolls 'em for you, you ain't apt to gain a thing,
You'll never learn enough to stand alone."

The Palo Duro country is as rough as it can be.
But sure is great for cattle when it's green.
The calves were big and soggy; them old cows were slick
    and fat.
The best year anyone had ever seen.

The stocker price was on the rise, near eighty cents a pound.
The last two years were hot and dry and lean.
The boss said, "This could be the time when we take up
    the slack,
So boys be sure you pick this pasture clean."

I saddled up the sorrel horse and he had come undone.
Tried every trick he knew to get me throwed.
He took the bit between this teeth and left there on the run
Jumpin' every bush and cactus in the road.

I thot if I'd just let him run, he'd finally settle down.
Boy, was I wrong, he never slowed his stride.
The boss just laughed as I went by, said, "Let him have
  his head,
We'll catch 'im when you reach the other side."

I took the outside circle in the Cita Canyon breaks.
The canyon walls are steep and twice as high.
They rise up from the valley floor about 300 feet.
The easy way to cross is learn to fly.

I topped out on a mesa just above a water hole.
The seep was marshy; wasn't very wide.
A cow was bogged up to her gut, but I can't go
  down there.
Why, that would be committing suicide.

I'm talkin' scared, I'm by myself, and tempted to go down.
I better add up all my options first.
What if he falls and I get hurt? I'd be down there for days.
What if I break my leg and die of thirst?

Besides all that, what's one old cow? We got 8,000 more.
Why risk my life to save that crazy thing?
They say we lose a couple every winter anyhow.
No one will even miss her till the spring.

And then I see a baldy calf a'hidin' in the brush.
The cow is talkin' to him loud and clear.
I know that any minute now he'll walk right in that bog,
We'll lose them both and me just settin' here.

I nudged the sorrel with my spurs, and he went off
  the edge,
Both forefeet planted, slidin' down the hill.
He picked his way among the rocks, sure footed
  as a goat.
Was scary but the trip was quite a thrill.

I never would believe that this old horse could be
  this good.
I never would have cussed him had I known
That he was good for anything but tearin' up the sod,
And doin' all he could to get me thrown.

We got down to the bottom and the calf run in the brush.
I roped the cow, the sorrel pulled her out.
I realized then he's my pardner—we made quite a team.
I stroked his neck and then I heard the shout.

The boys were lined up on the hill, a'givin' hoots
  and howls.
I guess they must have seen the entire show.
I wonder what they'd think of me if I'd stayed on the hill.
I didn't, so I guess I'll never know.

There were times I got so scared I almost write it off.
I nearly quit the outfit once or twice.
You got to pay the fiddler if you want to learn to dance.
That rocky ride was worth the fiddler's price.

The sorrel's gone to glory and now I'm the wagon boss.
My life's been good; I'm thankful for the ride.
Tho' there's been lots of rocky slopes to test a
  feller's nerves,
The fun's been climbin' out the other side.

1994

MY BEST FRIEND

Our hearts are entwined
Our lives are combined
We both understand what it means
To return to the place
Of our youthful embrace
And fulfill a lifetime of dreams.

The friends we hold dear
Our family is here
To share in our union of life
The vows that are spoken
Aren't meant to be broken
They're sacred to husband and wife.

We may disagree
But I'll try to see
Your side and not be demanding
If I get out of hand
And I take a strong stand
Promise you'll be understanding

I know there'll be times
When you'll be inclined
Just simply to give up the ghost
But remember sweet dove
That I'm hardest to love
At times when I need love the most.

It's my earnest prayer
You'll always be there
To share in my life till the end
And I want you to know
That wherever I go
You always will be my best friend.

*Written especially for Bill and Linda White on their
wedding day, February 16, 1991*

THE FENCE THAT ME AND SHORTY BUILT

We'd picked up all the fencing tools
And staples off the road.
An extra roll of 'bob' wire
Was the last thing left to load.

I drew a sleeve across my face
To wipe away the dirt.
The young man who was helping me
Was tuckin' in his shirt.

I turned around to him and said,
"This fence is finally done,
With five new strands of 'bob' wire
Shinin' proudly in the sun.

"The wire is runnin' straight and tight
With every post in line.
The kinda job you're proud of.
One that stands the test of time."

The kid was not impressed at all,
He stared off into space.
Reminded me of years ago,
Another time and place.

When I called myself a cowboy,
I was full of buck and bawl
I didn't think my hands would fit
Post augers and a maul.

But they sent me out with Shorty
And the ranch fence building crew.
Well, I was quite insulted
And before the day was through,

I let him know that I'm a cowboy,
This ain't what I do.
I ain't no dadgummed nester,
I hired out to buckaroo.

He said, "We'll talk about that son,
When we get in tonight.
Right now you pick them augers up.
It's either that or fight."

Boy, I was diggin' post holes
Faster than a Georgia mole.
But if a rock got in my way
I simply moved the hole.

So when the cowboys set the posts,
The line went in and out.
Old Shorty's face got fiery red
And I can hear him shout.

"Nobody but a fool would build
A fence that isn't straight.
I got no use for someone who ain't
Pullin' his own weight."

Well I thought for sure he'd hit me
Glad he didn't have a gun.
I looked around to find a place
Where I could duck and run.

But Shorty walked up to me
Just as calm as he could be.
Said, "Son, I need to talk to you,
Let's find ourselves a tree."

He rolled a Bull Durham cigarette
As we sat on the ground.
He took himself a puff or two
Then slowly looked around.

"Son, I ain't much on schoolin',
Didn't get too far with that.
But there's a lot of learnin'
Hidden underneath this hat.

"I got it all the hard way,
Every bump and bruise and fall.
Now some of it was easy,
But then most weren't fun a'tall.

"But one thing that I always got
From every job I've done,
Is do the best I can each day
And try to make it fun.

"I know that bustin' through them rocks
Ain't what you like to do.
By gettin' mad you've made it tough
On me and all the crew.

"Now you hired on to cowboy
And you think you've got the stuff.
You told him you're a good hand
And the boss has called your bluff.

"So how's that gonna make you look
When he comes ridin' through,
And he asks me who dug them holes
And I say it was you.

"Now we could let it go like this
And take the easy route.
But doin' things the easy way
Ain't what it's all about.

"The boss expects a job well done,
From every man he's hired.
He'll let you slide by once or twice,
Then one day you'll get fired.

"If you're not proud of what you do,
You won't amount to much.
You'll bounce around from job to job
Just slightly out of touch.

"Come mornin' let's re-dig those holes
And get that fence in line.
And you and I will save two jobs,
Those bein' yours and mine.

"And someday you'll come ridin' through
And look across this land,
And see a fence that's laid out straight
And know you had a hand,

"In something that's withstood the years.
Then proud and free from guilt,
You'll smile and say, 'Boys, that's the fence
That me and Shorty built.'"

1993

BrIGHT COManCHE MOOn

We gathered at Brown's cabin in the Brazos River
  Breaks.
We's all stirred up about an Injun raid.
Was early in December, the Comanche Moon was full,
The Parker County settlers were afraid.

The raiders were Nocona and his fierce Kwahadi band.
Out near the Palo Pinto County line
They killed a Mrs. Sherman and run off a lot of stock.
They took a dandy iron-gray horse of mine.

That geldin' was a good one, the best I've ever owned,
Kentucky bred and faster than the wind.
Pa brought him here to Texas when we come from
  Tennessee.
I'd ride through hell to get him back again.

We wasn't very organized, just rough-hewn volunteers,
But we was used to livin' in the wild.
Tho' Goodnight was a seasoned hand, he just turned
  twenty-four,
And barely fifteen, I was still a child.

I'd never faced an Injun, but my blood was fairly up,
And all the boys was spoilin' for a fight.
I think down deep I'se wishin' that them varmints would
  escape,
I shore warn't keen on fightin' 'em at night.

We cut their sign next mornin' just beyond Ioni Creek.
The band split up to throw us off the track.
We took the trail that headed west, but I kept on the watch,
Afraid the other bunch would double back.

Now Goodnight was a Ranger and he knew the country
  well.
He took the point and rode on up ahead.
In seven days we found their camp where Mule Crick
  hits the Pease.
Them Injuns was just gettin' out of bed.

We hit the camp arunnin'—Captain Ross was in the
  lead.
They scattered just like coyotes in the brush.
We rode through fires and teepees, shootin' everything
  that moved,
Creating mass confusion in the rush.

I saw some riders headed for a stand of cottonwoods,
A woman was aboard my good iron-gray.
She's ridin' like a demon and was carryin' a child.
I caught her just before she got away.

We had them Injuns sittin' in a circle on the ground,
All squaws and children, 'cept for one or two.
I seen the one that I had caught and did a double take.
When she looked up, I seen her eyes were blue.

We's lookin' for white captives 'cause they always take a
  few.
I pointed to the one that I had found.
We talked to her in English, but she didn't understand,
Just sat there moanin', starin' at the ground.

Then Sul Ross turned to me and said, "Might be that
  Parker girl."
We took her to Camp Cooper in a van.
We sent for Colonel Parker, and when he called out her
  name,
She stood straight up and said, "me Cincee Ann."

They took her then to Birdville where her Uncle Isaac
   lived.
She never readjusted to the life.
They say she died a'grievin' for her husband and her
   boys.
That woman was old Chief Nocona's wife.

Her first son, Quanah Parker, was the terror of the
   plains,
A savage, brutal warrior in his day.
He's up in Oklahoma now and walks the white man's
   road,
And me, I'm workin' cattle on my gray.

But I can't help but wonder if we done that woman
   wrong.
But we were certain we were right back then.
No way could we imagine she was better off out there.
To us they were barbaric, heathen men.

We settled in this county just before the Civil War—
Hard workin' people, full of hopes and dreams.
We saw the brutal massacres, we buried young and old,
We still remember savage, fiendish screams.

And in that stand of live oak trees are ghostly charred
   remains,
A family lived in constant fear and dread.
A solitary chimney built by hardy pioneers,
A solemn silent sentinel of the dead.

The north wind's gettin' nippy and the leaves are turnin'
   gold.
White snow geese signal winter's comin' soon.
Now we no longer live in fear and I look forward to
The autumn and its bright Comanche Moon.

1992

THE WeaTHer

There's something about a cool October mornin'
That suits my disposition just right.
The sky is as clear as a crystal today
and as the sun slowly creeps into sight.

My old pony's step is a little bit lighter
Must be the crisp Autumn air.
Cold weather's comin', no doubt about that,
He's growed a half inch of long hair.

I just saw some geese headin' south for the winter.
That shore is a beautiful sight.
Something inside of me stirs at the sound
of Canadian Honkers in flight.

The pronghorn are startin' to gather in bunches.
A sign winter's well on her way.
The mesquite trees have put on a good crop of beans,
Be a tough one the old timers say.

The boys and I cleared eighty acres of pasture.
We laid in 'bout ten cord of wood.
Burnin' mesquite is the cowboy's perfume,
Makes that musty old cabin smell good.

In the evening the missus will stoke up the fire
When it's cold and the snow drifts are deep,
We like to read but I only get through two pages
'Fore my old mind drifts off to sleep.

Lately I've noticed some pain in my joints,
Gets worse as the weather gets cold.
The Doc says I need to go someplace that's warm,
But shoot, it's just age taking hold.

My neighbor, he got him a place down in Scottsdale.
He leaves here before the first snow.
There ain't no way in hell I could go to the desert,
Wouldn't last maybe three days or so,

'Cause I'd get to missin' my chores in the winter
I get up every morning at five.
And I'd worry that if I wasn't right here to feed 'em,
There's a chance that my cows won't survive.

I'm right partial to cows, I'm there when they're calvin'.
The missus gives each one a name.
When they're older we cull 'em and thin out the dinks,
But when they're babies they all look the same.

Most people seem to like springtime the best,
When everything's fresh, clean, and clear.
But fall seems to say, hey, it's time to slow down
You've worked hard enough for one year.

I look forward to April—there's one special place,
Where I planted bluebonnets last year.
I hope they come up, they're my wife's favorite flower,
That's one reason I like it out here.

Listen to me, I'm just ramblin' around
Wouldn't change things if I had the chance.
The weather don't matter, I ain't goin' nowhere
There's no place I'd trade for this ranch.

1989

RIDe FOr THe BranD

His skin looked like leather.
He walked with a limp.
And talked with a slow Texas drawl.
His knuckles were knotted,
His left thumb was gone,
Said a stud bit it off late last fall.

We knew he was lyin'.
We watched him dally it up,
But it ain't healthy to call him a liar.
It was Saturday night
Before the wagon went out,
And he was settin' this new kid on fire.

Now we've all heard his stories
'Bout places he's been—
We all think that Jake's pretty strange.
He looked over at me,
Said, "I'm schoolin' this boy
'Bout the unwritten laws of the range."

The kid was enthralled,
Kinda like in a trance.
Jake sensed that he had a good grip.
He straightened up, hitched his pants,
Took a drink of cold beer,
Turned around with his hand on his hip.

He said, "Son, a man's brand
Is his own special mark
That says this is mine, leave it alone.
You hire out to a man,
Ride for his brand
And protect it like it was your own."

He said, "Mr. Waggoner
Come out here in 1903.
This country was sagebrush, mesquite trees, and sand.
He carved him this ranch,
Outa blood, sweat, and guts
So be proud that you ride for his brand.

"If you hire out to string bob wire,
Then build him a fence.
Don't matter if it's four or five strand.
Remember it was you
Who asked for the job,
So don't bitch when you ride for this brand.

"Mr. Waggoner don't
Hold with complainers
He'll fire one before he can quit.
So if you don't like our outfit,
Then head down the trail
Find a hoss that your saddle will fit.

"But if you get up early
And catch your own bronc
Show the boss that you're makin' a hand.
Mr. Waggoner'll be there
To cover your bets
As long as you ride for his brand."

He said, "The winter I spent
At the Sixes,
We had a man at the old Taylor place.
He rode up on some hiders,
A skinnin' a cow,
And squared off at them scamps face to face.

"Now he coulda rode off,
Never looked back.
But he just wasn't that kind of man.
We found him in Ash Creek,
Shot all to hell
Nocona Joe died for the brand."

We know the old man
Tells a windy or two.
Like the one about losing his thumb.
And Nocona was killed,
In a bar in Fort Worth,
By the demons in a bottle of rum.

But I got to thinkin',
'bout what he had said.
And the more of it I understand.
The more I believe,
We'd be all better off
If more people would Ride for the Brand.

1987

THE SONG OF THE WEST

I'm ridin' a pasture I've never been in
Where the cattle are brush-wise and wild.
Rode up on some headstones out here on the ridge;
There's a man and his wife and a child.

There's not a foundation. I've looked all around.
No sign of a house here at all.
No fence posts and "bob" wire, no old wagon parts,
No trace of a barn or a stall.

I looked all around for the sign of a town,
But the base of the ridge is all clear.
So why were they buried on top of this hill.
Did something real bad happen here?

Were they part of a wagon train headed out west
When the cholera struck 'em all down?
Or did they try to cross when the river was high;
Went under and all of 'em drowned?

Perhaps they were trailin' out here all alone
To a homestead, the land of their dreams,
When the Kiowa came out of nowhere that day,
Did they die to the sound of their screams?

Way down in the valley, I see some flat ground
Where a man could have turned up some sod.
I don't understand why 'cause it's dry as a bone,
But the nesters trust those things to God.

Could be they was ranchers, the last of their breed.
They first saw their claim from this hill.
They made their kids promise to bring 'em back here
Where they're spendin' eternity, still.

It took all kinds of people to settle this land.
The hardy, the good, and the best.
But whoever they were and whatever they did,
They're a verse in the song of the west.

1994

THE PICTURE

The little frame house in the cottonwood trees
Looks the same as when I was a kid.
I slept on the porch on those hot summer nights,
Because that's what my grandfather did.

Grandpa was a cowboy, my hero and friend,
And I thought he was twenty foot tall.
I dogged out his footsteps from morning till night,
Then I went back to school in the fall.

He worked on the Matador when he was young,
And the Four Sixes Panhandle branch.
He came back to Weatherford, married Grandma,
And they bought this old hardscrabble ranch.

Each day was a struggle they somehow got by,
Tho' the banker owned most of their stock.
They raised Longhorn cows and a houseful of kids
On mesquite brush and cedar and rock.

His old spinster sister has just passed away,
And she left me a bunch of her stuff—
A big box of pictures of him and Grandma,
And a case of Four Dot Garrett Snuff.

I drove out this morning to show them these things,
And identify all of my kin,
So they become people with faces and names,
Like a cousin or old family friend.

Grandma was tickled, and she knew every face.
She'd name 'em and I'd written 'em down.
Grandpa in his rocker just fooled with his hat,
He kept changing the crease in the crown.

Was one in particular she studied hard.
It was her and Grandpa on this place.
Her calico dress was a sign of the times,
And his hat covered most of his face.

Dry cowhides were hanging across the top rail.
That's all they had left from the drought.
She said, "Look here, Pa, you remember this year
Was the summer we nearly pulled out."

He put on his glasses and laid down his hat,
Then he stared at the picture awhile.
He squinted his eyes and then looked up at her,
And he answered in true cowboy style.

"That black bald-faced pony, that's Curly Wolf,
That renegade, jugheaded runt.
The stockin' legged pony is old Santy Claus.
But, Ma, who are these people in front?"

1991

THE Maverick Way

A maverick's never worn a brand,
At least not one that shows.
He's free to travel where he will,
The trail is one he chose.

A stray is one who's been a part
of someone else's band,
And drifted to another range,
But he still wears the brand.

His leaders cry, "You've lost your mind,
That's not the way it's done.
A chosen few can make that move
You don't look like the one."

Then safe inside the pasture fence
Afraid to stand alone,
Unsure of his opinions, he's
No longer on his own.

Now what if all the skeptics had
Discouraged Ford and Bell,
Or Roosevelt said, "Let's don't fight,"
The day Pearl Harbor fell?

If Jonas Salk had not come up
With polio vaccine,
Or some bright mind had not perceived
The television screen?

The mavericks make a difference. They
Know where to find the feed.
They don't cry out "Take care of me,
The grass has gone to seed."

The tough times make them buckle up
And bow their necks and pull.
They never lay their shovel down
Until their bucket's full.

If I appear a renegade
And don't conform to style,
Don't think me strange or crazy, just
Ride down my trail awhile.

But if I choose a path that you
Find rocky, rough, or steep,
The herd has left an easy trail
The ruts are wide and deep.

Remember, nothing ever grows
Till someone plants a seed.
The scenery changes only
For the steer that's in the lead.

So try to use your talents so
That some kind soul will say,
"That feller there's a maverick, he
Ain't just your average stray."

1990

THE SHANK OF THE EVENIN'

That new batch of heifers we got in today
Come off of the truck in a run.
They scattered and split like a covey of quail.
We're lucky, we found every one.

Got talked into them by a trader last week.
I wonder if I'm still the boss.
South Georgia can keep all them rats with long ears
I like Hereford and Black Angus cross.

The grass in the meadow is starting to burn,
Gets brown just a little each day.
If we get a rain by the end of the month
I'd still get a cutting of hay.

We got a good shower the middle of March.
Was dry as a bone up till then.
It's the third week of June, we ain't had one since,
It may never rain here again.

I guess if I'se up to my stirrups in mud
I'd think there's a drought on the way.
If it rains for a week, it still ain't enough,
I'm lookin' for clouds every day.

I'm grateful as hell for the moisture I get.
I reckon I get my fair share.
But I like my mama cows rollin' in fat.
Without rain they're nothin' but hair.

The breeze 'cross the back porch is coolin' things down.
My yeller dog's lickin' my hand.
He knows when I worry 'bout cattle and rain.
No one but him understands.

The coyotes are startin' to yip at the moon.
The yeller dog joins in the fun
He's brave as a bear when they're out on the hill.
They challenge him, he'll turn and run.

Hey, life ain't so tough, we got our own place,
The missus ain't cranky with me.
The kids are all growed up and gone off to school.
We're happy as we want to be.

Yes, this time of day is real special to me.
It's when I reshuffle my load.
I add it all up, and come out way ahead,
When daylite's been saucered and blowed.

In the shank of the evenin' I boil it all down
To the basics, there ain't nothin' more.
We've got a good life and we like it out here.
The tough times just even the score.

We could sell this old homestead and move into town,
But what in the hell would I do
In the shank of the evenin', fight traffic and noise?
No thank you, I'll tough this one through.

1990

ALL THEY'VE CHANGED IS THE GUARD
AT FORT SILL

The Wichita Mountains rise out of the haze.
I imagine the sounds of a drill.
But all that I hear is a meadowlark's song.
The parade ground is ghostly and still.

There's lots of activity 'round the old fort—
The modern, mechanical kind.
But my mind has taken me back through the years,
To a colorful, romantic time.

The days when the horse corral, full of good stock,
Was fit for the winter campaign,
And the troopers rode out in columns of two
For another assault on the plain.

The rattle of sabers, the sergeant's commands,
The clank of the traces and chains,
The creak of the leather, the clatter of hooves—
Oh! the feel of the saddle and reins.

Below the Red River clear down to the coast,
Quanah Parker is at it again,
Leaving a path of destruction and death,
Killing women and children and men.

The wires fairly buzz on the telegraph poles,
Sending messages all through the fall.
Sherman and Sheridan, Buell and Miles—
All readily answer the call.

Ranald McKenzie has chased the Comanches
All summer, the campaign is tough.
Late in September, he finds them encamped
At the base of a high canyon bluff.

Spotting the camp and descending the wall
Of the Indians' ancient stronghold.
He cuts off the pony herd, kills every one;
Leaves the people afoot in the cold.

Beaten and hungry, they finally come in.
Quanah surrenders his arms.
He lives to see all of the great western plain
Broken up into ranches and farms.

The scourge of New Mexico finally is caught.
While the infantry march on parade,
The wily Geronimo, caged like a wolf,
Walks a cell in the old post stockade.

The silence is shattered, my journey is marred.
By the sounds of the wakening crowd.
I wonder what Sherman would think of the noise?
Bet he'd think it was vulgar and loud.

The settlement of the American West
Was a clash of two cultures of men.
It's sad that it's taken a hundred long years
For old enemies to become friends.

These men are still guarding American soil,
And, God willing, these men always will.
Their mission the same, keep America free.
All they've changed is the guard at Fort Sill.

1990

THE BELL ON OLD BLUE

Let me tell you a story 'bout a tarnished old bell
One we'd all like to hear ring again.
A graphic reminder of the glorious West
And of horses and cattle and men.

It hung 'round the neck of an old Goodnight steer
The big one the cowboys called Blue.
The Colonel had got him on the Bosque from Chisum
In the winter of '72.

The colonel sent thousands of steers up the trail
They learned to follow that bell day and night.
So at sundown the boss put a strap on the clapper
So the steers would stay bedded and quiet.

'Cause if old Blue got restless and started to roam
There'd be a stampede sure as hell.
The cattle would immediately be on their feet
And move toward the sound of the bell.

I remember a camp out on seven mile hill
In the distance were the Dodge City lights.
'Bout midnight it started to stormin' like hell
And lightning balls danced in the night.

The Boss yelled, "Find Blue and undo the clapper.
Git 'em up, string 'em out on the trail."
Blue swam the river, headed straight for the yards,
With 2,000 steers on his tail.

Well, the rail cars were loaded and we headed 'er south
The boys stayed in Dodge 'cept a few.
Like me and Frank Mitchell and Club-Footed Jack
We took the wagon, the remuda, and Blue.

The sky seemed lots bluer back out on the trail
Through the range where buffalo roam.
And where the dust devils dance their waltz with the wind
Old Blue was a-leadin' us home.

Blue was turned out at the Quitaque Ranch
Like a gentleman, pampered in style.
But we'd occasionally neck him to an old outlaw steer
Blue loved that, he'd drag him ten mile.

When the Lord called old Blue up that trail in the sky
The colonel had us cut off his horns.
He said, "Blue don't need 'em and they'll remind us of him
and trail drives, and stampedes, and storms."

Well, we still work cattle, we don't trail 'em to Dodge
'Cause fences now stand in the way.
And the Colonel he's ridin' that trail in the sky
But his cowboys still brand the JA.

As I reminisce I'm reminded that I am
One of the fortunate few
Who's had the privilege of hearin' a night herder's song
And the sound of that bell on old Blue.

1989

BOLEY

The first time I met Boley I was seven, maybe eight.
He sold my dad a set of longhorn steers.
About the time that school was out I helped him brand
   his calves.
I worked for Boley six or seven years.

He traded for a pinto colt the day that I turned twelve.
He helped me break him, taught me how to ride.
After that I dogged his footsteps everywhere he went.
He couldn't lose me even if he tried.

Old Boley rode the finest horses I had ever seen.
He never seemed to keep 'em very long.
He'd trade 'em off then leave awhile and bring some new
   ones home.
I never dreamed he's doing something wrong.

We lived in Palo Pinto and his place was south of town.
He branded lots of cattle every spring.
I often thought it funny that he didn't own a cow.
But I kept quiet and didn't say a thing.

He had an army contract and he sold the neighbors some.
But yet each year his steer herd multiplied.
All those years he's strippin' bull calves off the neighbor's
   cows.
My daddy told me after Boley died.

I'se sittin' on the courthouse lawn with Burt and
   Billy Joe—
Their folks was testifying at a trial.
My daddy and the Sheriff asked if Boley was in town.
I said, "No sir, he's been gone for quite a while."

Early that next mornin' they all gathered at our house.
They held a secret meeting in the den.
I hunkered down outside the door and listened to them talk.
They was saying bad things 'bout my friend.

The sheriff said that Boley was a rustler and a thief;
He'd stole some calves from Mr. Slaughter's herd.
Last week he took a gelding from a man in Fredericksburg.
They're lyin' and I don't believe a word.

I saddled up my pinto and rode out to Boley's place.
I got to let him know they're on his trail.
I figured I'd go with him all the way to Mexico.
I never thought I might wind up in jail.

Boley's place was empty, 'cept for one horse in the barn,
A sorrel mare he used to let me ride.
From the looks of things he hadn't been at home for
  several days.
I left a note before I walked outside.

And then I saw the posse as they raced across the hill;
Boley out in front a'ridin' hard.
He slid his pony to a stop and got off next to me,
Then raised his hands as they rode in the yard.

Now if I hadn't been there, Boley might have got away.
His horse was yet responding to the quirt.
He knew that I admired him, and I'm certain that he
  sensed
I might do something stupid and get hurt.

His trial didn't last too long, was too much evidence.
They hung him on July the 23rd.
I was on the front row and his eyes locked into mine.
He ducked his head and didn't say a word.

Boley had a lot of friends who came to say good-bye.
I went to pay my last respects, of course.
My daddy said, "One thing for sure, he's always
   mounted good.
A shame it had to be a borrowed horse."

1995

THE VISALIA

A friend of mine who raises horses asked if I would stay
And halter break some yearlin's in the fall.
We'd finished eatin' supper, I was leaned back in a chair,
As I watched the fire cast shadows on the wall,

I heard his footsteps on the porch before I heard him knock.
My friend yelled out "Old pardner come on in."
He'd seen him comin' up the drive and recognized the truck,
And knew the lanky cowboy was a friend.

His weathered features, gnarled hands, and bent
   bowlegged walk
All told of life out on the open plain.
His dress was plain and simple but he held his head up high.
With hat in hand he told us why he came.

He said he needed horses that could handle rocky ground.
They had to have good feet and big and stout.
Where he was headed, cattle were untouched by
   human hands.
They's payin' by the head to clean 'em out.

He said he had no money, just a promise that he'd pay,
A chance he wouldn't turn a dime till spring.
He didn't want to borrow mounts; he'd probably wear 'em out
Said when he's through they won't be worth a thing.

My friend said, "Go out to the barn and talk to Esquivel,
He's got 'em up this evenin' in the pen.
There'll be a bunch of good ones, take as many as you need.
I'll see you when you get your cattle in."

He went out to his pickup for a moment and returned,
An old Visalia saddle in his hand.
He sat it on a barrel, as he turned to walk away,
Said, "I'll be back to get this when I can."

"Old pard," I said, "That ain't much loot for what them
  horses cost.
I think you got the wrong end of this deal.
That old saddle ain't worth nothing." He turned to me
  and said
"To tell the truth my friend, I got a steal.

"I ain't worried 'bout my horses, you just saw an honest man.
His granddad rode that saddle up the trail.
He intends to keep his promise, this is just for me to hold.
He knows I know that saddle ain't for sale.

"And if it takes him twenty years he'll get that saddle back.
He'll whittle at the debt until it's right.
An honest man will break his back protecting his good name.
A thief will fade away into the night.

"You see the way he held himself with head and shoulders
  high
No doubt he carries his share of the load
He values that old saddle 'bout as much as life itself
And I am proud to help him down the road.

"My granddad came to Texas just before the Civil War
When cash was scarce and land was wild and free
Was known to always help a man who tried to help himself.
I hope that some of that rubbed off on me."

The lesson that I learned that night is still with me today—
Don't be afraid to stand out from the herd.
You'll be repaid ten thousand times with pride and
  self-respect
While other folks place value on your word.

I didn't stay that winter; wasn't much for me to do.
I worked the yearlin's and went on my way.
After several years I heard my friend has gone to his reward
I came down for the service yesterday.

I walked into the cabin to relive some happy times.
I looked for that old saddle everywhere.
In the corner was the barrel where he laid it years ago;
Was empty, that old saddle wasn't there.

Inside the church we whispered and remembered our
  old friend.
The preacher helped us all to recollect,
And over in the corner sat a solitary man
With hat in hand, he paid his last respects.

I never got to ask him if he got his saddle back
I'll bet my Justin boots he made the trade
And when he goes to rope in that big round-up in the sky
the Lord will say, "Your entry fees are paid."

1999

For J.J.

A lanky cowboy standin' hipshot just outside the
   gate,
Is waitin' for the word to come on in.
St. Peter says the gate's wide open, make yourself at
   home,
You'll want to see your family and your friends.

Your mom and dad are in that wagon comin' up the
   lane,
There's Lottie, Thurston, Neely, Hazel, Joe.
Merrick's on the saddle horse, he's bringin' one for
   you,
They've come to greet you and to take you home.

George is ridin' Hollywood, Miss Anne is by his side
She's on the stallion golden as the sun.
Mr. Tom is with the cowboys ridin' good 4-6s stock
They'll come by to howdy one by one.

St. Peter said we've got some cattle hidin' in the
   brush.
We've stirred 'em up for nigh 200 years.
We got some real good cowboys and they give it all
   they got,
But the Lord said put it off till you got here.

The wagon's staked out by the creek, Joe's got the
   coffee on.
The men are saddled ready for the ride.
They'll wait for you to drop them off then flush the
   wild ones out.
They know the right man's headin' up the drive.

There's never been a cowboy with the savvy that
   you've got.
The way you handle stock and men as well.
Everyone who knows you gives you nothing but
   respect,
And they're all glad to see you, you can tell.

That's your string of horses standin' over by the
   rail.
They're hand picked by the master just for you.
Don't worry 'bout a ruckus, they've forgotten how
   to buck,
You've got some favorites, Tonk and Frisco Blue.

The weather's perfect all year long, it never sleets
   or snows.
The sky is crystal clear and royal blue.
We're never in a hurry and we brand the whole year
   round.
We love it 'cause we can't tell when we're through.

We had a shower this morning, 'cause we get one every day,
We never have to worry 'bout a rain.
The grass is lush and stirrup high, the cattle slick
   and fat,
We're not concerned with weaning, weights, and gains.

All you ever wanted was to be a 6s hand.
You've been a good one, you're not nearly through.
Your crew's already saddled and they're ready for the ride.
Some you learned from, some that learned from you.

Naida made your world complete, the perfect friend
  and wife.
And you are more than proud of Mike and Jim.
With little J.J. on the way and P.L. growing strong
The legacy you left will live with them.

You thought you were in heaven every day since you
  were born.
So we made sure that nothing here has changed.
Work cattle to your heart's content and visit with
  your friends,
You're now at home on heaven's open range.

Welcome J.J.

2001

THE BLUE ROAN AND THE KID

The kid was in the round pen saddlin' up a blue roan colt.
The horse reared back and throwed a wall-eyed fit.
A horse with any sense will fight awhile then give it up,
But this one was the kind that wouldn't quit.

The kid hauled off and kicked him in the belly and
    the flank;
Just then the lead rope give and snapped in two.
The colt run in a corner; stood there snortin' like a hog.
The kid was usin' every word he knew.

I almost climbed the fence and give that boy a talkin' to.
But something told me, let him play his hand.
You'd only make it worse by jumping on him when
    he's mad.
He'd have to fight you just to make a stand.

The kid shook out his catch rope when the pony broke
    and run.
He caught both forefeet, then took up the slack.
The colt fell on his shoulder and then landed in a heap.
He hit so hard I thought it broke his back.

He slipped the bridle on his head then flogged him with
    his rope.
The wind was filled with dust and flying hair.
And then he let the horse get up and pulled his
    head around
And swung into the saddle light as air.

That blue roan throwed him higher than a full grown
    cottonwood.
The thud was sickening when he hit the ground.
I climbed the fence to see if he was dead or just out cold.
Except for loss of air the kid was sound.

Then when he finally got his air the kid looked up at me
And said, "I finally found one I can't ride.
I thought I had that sucker broke and ready for the bit.
I wouldn't give you two bits for his hide."

"Oh," I said, "you'd be surprised what tenderness can do.
You young bucks try to do it all today.
Go take your saddle off that colt and let him blow awhile
Before you let a good one get away.

"Son, it don't come that easy, it takes lots of work
   and time.
All you lose when you git throwed is pride.
You cull the ones that you can't ride the first time
   you get on,
There'll soon be nothin' left for you to ride."

He walked off to the bunkhouse with his pride as low
   as dirt.
I wondered if I'd been a little rough.
But later on this afternoon he'll have a different view,
And maybe life won't seem so cold and tough.

My daddy was the kind of man that wouldn't let you quit.
He'd drive you till you wouldn't drive no more.
If it hadn't been for Mama, I'd have turned to outlaw ways.
Glad she was there to even up the score.

I swore that I would raise my son to have a gentle hand.
Time will tell, but Lord knows that I've tried,
He didn't have no mama, see I raised him by myself.
The kid was born the day his mama died.

I guess it kind of scared me when I seen him flog that horse.
I thought I'd failed in what I'd tried to do.
I'm glad I held my temper 'cause when you fight fire
   with fire
All you do is burn your fingers too.

I guess he must'a listened 'cause I saw him late today
Along the river south of Jackson flat.
He was moving through the willows in a long ground-
    eatin' trot.
The roan was actin' gentle as a cat.

If a feller is cantankerous and he likes to argue some,
I don't cull him just because we disagree.
But if he treats his horses with contempt and disrespect,
I figure that's the way that he'll treat me.

That's why it's so important for that kid to show respect
And learn to answer for his own mistakes.
If not, he'll lay his failures off on everybody else,
Then claim he lost because he got bad breaks.

1995

WHEN JOSEPH WAS CHIEF

From the long winding valley where teepees once stood
The mountains rise lofty and steep.
I envisioned a pony herd grazing the hills.
The camp was at peace and asleep.

And then I imagined the thunder of hooves
As soldiers rode over the hill.
Bodies lay scattered all over the ground,
And the voice of a people was still.

A few of the lucky ones fled to the hills.
They were hungry with no place to go.
The great chief was saddened, his people were cold.
He surrendered his lance and his bow.

The great leader Chief Joseph ruled not by the hand,
But by examples of wisdom and deeds.
The good of his people was first in his thoughts.
His decisions were based on their needs.

We told him his God was not equal to ours.
We lied, we bred hate and distrust.
We set out to annihilate a whole race of man,
And make him over in the image of us.

It would not have been easy to live side by side,
But the truth is that we didn't try.
And it seems inhumane and so senseless to me,
For the women and children to die.

Why did we chain him in a cage like a wolf,
Make him feel less than a man?
Move him to ground unfamiliar and strange,
Trade death and disease for his land?

It's doubtful the nations can ever be free,
'Cause the people are broken and weak.
But I hope that somewhere in a sweat lodge tonight
A young man hears his true spirit speak.

He'll know that the old ways can never be lost,
That he must rekindle the light.
As I think of all the injustice, I feel
The Great Spirit is listening tonight.

I ask him to hear all the suffering and pain
Be watchful of all of his kin.
Then help us remember to live and let live
Before it happens all over again.

1989

TO AN OLD FRIEND

I stood by the fountain as they brought him in.
A lost lonely look on his face.
I ain't never seen him in nothin' but boots.
The wheelchair shore seemed out of place.

It took him a while to recall who I am,
but confusion turned into a grin.
It was tho' we were saddled up, ready to ride
The Hackberry Pasture again.

He laughed as he said, "I remember the time,
That yeller bronc swallered his head,
And pitched you so high that you turned over twice.
Me'n Benny Bob swore you was dead."

He looked up at me and asked, "How is old Ben?"
I lied and said, "He's doin' fine."
No need to remind him his brother was gone.
Ben died back in seventy-nine.

For most of an hour we rode at a trot.
We branded and shaped up the steers,
Drank gallons of coffee, ate sourdough bread,
and cowboyed for fifty-one years.

I thot he's an old man when I was a kid,
At a time when I needed a friend,
He took me to raise, taught me all that I know,
'Bout horses and cattle and men.

My daddy had died and I needed a job.
I'se big for a kid of fifteen.
They put me to work on the four 6s Ranch.
Was dumb as a gourd and as green.

We's lookin' for strays in the Wichita Breaks
Was me and John Gaither and him
I lost sight of John so I'se lookin' around
'A daydreamin' there on the rim.

Rode up on some cattle hid out in the brush
A two-year-old steer come by me,
Throwed a nine in his tail and cut a new trail
Right out through them salt cedar trees.

I took in behind him a givin' it hell
The colt I was ridin' was green
I thot to myself, he ain't getting away
This roan is a running machine.

Was goin' full bore when we got to the bank
The stream wasn't wide as my hat
I nearly pulled up, but I thot, What the Hell
I've jumped rivers wider than that.

I bogged that old pony plumb up to his gut
Was wallerin' and thrashin' around
He's goin' down deeper with each desperate lunge
Me prayin' he'd find solid ground.

Just at the moment that I heard his voice
A rope appeared right by the roan
"Get outa that kack and hang on to my line
The colt'll get out on his own."

I've crossed that old river a many a time
I've found me a bog once or twice.
But I still remember that thirty-foot rope
And this cowboy piece of advice.

"When you ride the river, son, make sure your horse
Is gentle and seasoned as well.
'Cause only the good ones will get you across.
That quicksand goes clean down to hell."

I got up to leave and he reached for my hand.
Said, "Son, I'm sure glad you dropped by.
If you see old Ben, have him saddle my horse,
I hate sittin' waitin' to die."

His voice started crackin', he swallered and said
"I'm nearin' the end of my ride
If I cross the river before you get there,
I'll leave a good horse on this side."

1990

Hats off to the cowboy

The city folks think that it's over.
The cowboy has outlived his time—
An old worn-out relic, a thing of the past,
But the truth is, he's still in his prime.

The cowboy's the image of freedom,
The hard-ridin' boss of the range.
His trade is a fair one, he fights for what's right,
And his ethics aren't subject to change.

He still tips his hat to the ladies,
Let's you water first at the pond.
He believes a day's pay is worth a day's work,
And his handshake and word are his bond.

1989

SOURDOUGH, BEEFSTEAK, AND BEANS

The top of my tarp sure is heavy this mornin',
These Pendleton blankets feel nice.
It's a good thing I stuck all my clothes in my bedroll,
The canvas is covered with ice.

I just stuck my hand out from under the covers.
The mornin' air sure has a bite.
It was warm as September when I went to bed,
Musta blowed up a norther last night.

The coosie's been rattlin' them ovens since four.
The horse wrangler's ready to ride.
I hear Buster and Bubba thrashin' around,
And I could git up if I tried.

But it's nice to just lay here in my warm canvas world,
And know that I'm one lucky man.
To be able to do what I like to do most,
A genuine workin' cowhand.

Yesterday I was ridin' old Toby.
I'se relaxed with my hands on my knees.
But I grabbed for the horn when a big golden eagle
Flew out of a cottonwood tree.

It shore was a sight when he took to the wing.
Caused me and old Toby to stop
And watch as the wind took him out 'cross the canyon,
Where he lit in a cedar on top.

Right after sunup, we jumped an old maverick.
I throwed at his horns and it stuck.
When Toby sat down and he hit the end of my line,
It felt like we'd roped us a truck.

He turned 'round and faced us, a-pawing the ground.
I thought, boy this is my lucky day.
Then he run up my rope like he's goin' to water,
We's dodgin' him every which way.

He come alongside, hooked a horn in my back cinch,
For a minute I thought he had won.
But Tobe didn't booger, he stayed right in stride
Until I got the buckle undone.

I'se tied hard and fast but I finally shook loose,
Snubbed him and left him all night.
I'll lead him in when we drive through the canyon.
This evenin' he's shore full of fight.

The wagon boss roped me old Peppy today,
And I know when I tighten my kack,
I better grab a deep seat 'cause he'll buck like a colt,
take a good hand to stay on his back.

I don't understand why a cold frosty mornin'
Makes a gentle horse break plumb in two.
Nothin' feels worse than to land on your face
With your buddies all laughin' at you.

I had a choice, coulda gone off to college,
So you probably think I'm a fool.
But out here I'm happy, I feel more alive,
And they don't teach you to cowboy in school.

Out here a man's word means he'll do what he says
And they don't make excuses for youth.
Ain't a bed in the bunkhouse for punchers who steal
Or someone who can't tell the truth.

You know why I do this? It's my way of life.
I'm at home in my wildrag and jeans.
And I ain't got no stomach for fancy French food.
Make mine sourdough, beefsteak, and beans.

Well, the wrangler just come in from jinglin' the horses.
Him and coosie are havin' a cup.
The smell of the coffee comes right through the canvas,
Guess I'd better get dressed and git up.

1989

we're hangin' him tonite

He was such a nice young feller
Came from good North Texas stock
Had a proper church upbringing
Family, solid as a rock.

But somewhere the boy got twisted
Heard the painted siren's song
On the streets of HELL'S HALF ACRE'S
Where they say the lad went wrong.

What a loss of time and talent
What a song to go unsung
Seems the fruits of life are wasted
On the foolish and the young.

Now he could have turned out different
Been a kind and decent man
But tonite his earthly judgment's
In the vigilante's hand.

And somewhere his mama's cryin'
As she prays by candlelight
She'll never hold her child again
'Cause we're hangin' him tonite.

1995

Paw-Paw

I called my granddad Paw-Paw and I loved him more than life.
I tried to copy everything he did.
'Course I was always underfoot and standing in the gate
But if I made him mad, he kept it hid.

When I was two he bought me my own saddle and a horse.
The seat of his old pickup was my bed.
I learned to walk the way he walked and cuss a little bit
I hung on every word my Paw-Paw said.

Paw-Paw used to brag on me to all the other guys.
Said I would be a champion someday.
He taught me how to ride a bronc when I was just a kid,
I wasn't good enough to make it pay.

So when my grandson came along I recognized the chance
To relive memories of my childhood days,
My daughter said that Paw-Paw wasn't very dignified,
But I had him call me Paw-Paw anyways.

I taught him how to throw a rope and he roped everything
That came in his imaginary pen.
I bought him his own saddle and a little spotted horse,
He and that horse became the best of friends.

I guess I overdid it 'cause he got us both in Dutch
When he caught grandma's rooster in his loop.
The rooster didn't make it and his grandma threw a fit
He said, "The old bird's tough, he'll make good soup."

We've dodged a bullet once or twice and we've come out OK.
Tho' we haven't gotten by with everything.
Like early last September we was branding April calves,
The ones too small to brand in early spring.

I'se way across the brandin' pens not paying him no mind,
I caught him in the corner of my eye.
He was in the pen a-foot and building him a loop
I chuckled to myself, the boy's got try.

Much to my surprise and his, he caught a heifer calf
That musta weighed at least four hundred pound
She jerked that youngster off his feet 'fore I could blink an eye,
She quit the herd and took to higher ground.

She drug him through the fresh manure and up against the fence.
His shirt was torn to tatters in the chase
His pants was hanging off his hips, his boots was full of dirt
But bless his heart his hat was still in place.

I double hocked the heifer and the groundcrew stretched her out.
The boy escaped, but Lord I don't know how.
I swear I nearly lost it when he said, "Build yourself a loop,
And let's go get ourselves another cow."

When we were in the barn last night he asked if he could rope.
I laughed it off and said, "I guess you can."
I never dreamed a four year old would have that kind of nerve
I'm sure the heifer didn't understand.

I said, "Let's ride down to the tank and wash your face and hands."
Then what he said just thrilled me though and through.
"But you don't wash your face and hands till you get in at night.
I wanna be a cowboy just like you."

The mighty hero had returned victorious from the war
The hand he held was flush and full of spades.
With cow manure on remnants of what used to be a shirt
He expected nothing less than accolades.

But unless you've fought the battle and unless you've won the war
The taste of victory don't seem quite so sweet.
His mama saw destruction and a bruised and battered boy.
To her his hard won victory spelled defeat.

He reveled in his glory as he told his mom the tale.
He said, "that heifer run right in my noose.
I worked her round the pen, till Paw-Paw caught her by the heels
We burned her hide before we cut her loose."

She said, "Why did you do that?" as she grabbed him by the arm.
I raised that girl and boy can she get mean.
Before I let him in too deep I'll throw the kid a line
Right now it's best that I ain't heard or seen.

We're talkin' 'bout a cyclone and a giant hissy fit,
If she reacted like I thought she would.
I popped the buttons off my shirt when he looked up and said,
"I did it 'cause my Paw-Paw said I could."

1995

THE WAGON TONGUE

Hired out to Colonel Slaughter drivin' steers to Abilene,
Green and wet behind the ears, a kid of seventeen.
Tho' I was raised in Texas, I was not a seasoned hand.
I got the job of hoodlum, the coosie's right-hand man.

On the Llano Estacado all you see is endless plain.
You dread the sound of thunder, there's no shelter from
　　the rain.
Our coosie did a strange thing when the evening meal
　　was done.
He'd wait until the stars came out, then move the
　　wagon tongue.

CHORUS

He said, "Son, there ain't no landmarks on these wide
　　and rolling plains.
There ain't no trees or mountains, so each day it looks
　　the same,
But you'll never lose direction, and you'll know just
　　where you are,
If you always point the wagon tongue towards the old
　　North Star.

Out beyond the Cimarron one cold and stormy night,
I saw the cattle stampede in the lightnin's eerie light.
Took several days to round 'em up and get 'em settled
　　down.
We followed with the wagon through the soft and
　　muddy ground.

As we pushed the herd across the plain, we had no way
　　to know
That we had drifted way off course toward New
　　Mexico.
And the night the stars came out, his theory stood the
　　test.
Abilene's up north of us, but we were headed west.

CHORUS

My life has been a full one, and my hair is turning gray.
I've seen a lot of sunshine, and I've seen some cloudy
  days.
For a while I wandered aimlessly, and I still wear the
  scars
When I didn't point my wagon tongue toward the old
  North Star.

SECOND CHORUS

Life is like a grassy sea, the trail ain't always plain.
One may lead to pleasure and the other lead to pain.
But you'll never lose direction and you'll know just
  where you are,
If you'll always point your wagon tongue toward your
  own north star.

1992

THE WAGON TONGUE

By Red Steagall

(1.) Hired out to Colo-nel Slaugh- ter driv-in' steers to A- bi-lene.
(2.) Lla- no Es-ta-ca- do all you see is o- pen plain.

(3) Green and wet be- hind the ears, a kid of sev-en-teen.
You dread the sound of thun-der, there's no shel- ter from the rain.

Tho' I was raised in Tex- as, I was
Our Coo-sie did a strange thing when the

not a sea- soned hand. I got the job of hood- lum, the
ev- ening meal was done. He'd wait un-til the stars came out, then

coo- sies right hand man. (2) On the He said, "Son, there ain't no
move the wa-gon tongue.

land-marks on these wide and roll- ing plains. There ain't no trees or moun-

-tains, so each day it looks the same, But you'll

ne- ver lose di- rec-tion, and you'll know just where you are, If you

al- ways point the wa- gon tongue t'wards the old North Star."

© 1992 Texas Red Songs

-79-

ACKNOWLEDGMENTS

"The Memories in Grandmother's Trunk," *Ride for the Brand: The Poetry and Songs of Red Steagall.* Fort Worth: Bunkhouse Press, 1993.

"The Code of the West Hasn't Changed," *Ride for the Brand: The Poetry and Songs of Red Steagall.* Copyright © 1992 Fred Fellows.

"A Dusty Cotton Field," *The Fence That Me and Shorty Built,* Fort Worth: Bunkhouse Press, 2001.

"Bedroll," *Ride for the Brand: The Poetry and Songs of Red Steagall.*

"McCorkle and the Wire," *Ride for the Brand: The Poetry and Songs of Red Steagall.* Copyright © 1992 Joe Beller.

"Born to This Land," *Ride for the Brand: The Poetry and Songs of Red Steagall; Born to this Land,* Poems by Red Steagall and Photographs by Skeeter Hagler. Lubbock: Texas Tech University Press, 2007.

"The Real America," *The Fence That Me and Shorty Built; Born to this Land.*

"Deacon and the Dun," *Ride for the Brand: The Poetry and Songs of Red Steagall.*

"The Last Buffalo," *Ride for the Brand: The Poetry and Songs of Red Steagall.*

"Climbin' Out the Other Side," *The Fence That Me and Shorty Built.*

"My Best Friend," previously unpublished.

"The Fence That Me and Shorty Built," *The Fence That Me and Shorty Built.*

"Bright Comanche Moon," *Ride for the Brand: The Poetry and Songs of Red Steagall.*